LET'S RIDE!

ATVS

MARIE ROGERS

PowerKiDS press

NEW YORK

Published in 2022 by The Rosen Publishing Group, Inc.
29 East 21st Street, New York, NY 10010

First Edition

Portions of this work were originally authored by J. Poolos and published as *Wild About ATVs*. All new material this edition authored by Marie Rogers.

Editor: Kate Mikoley
Book Design: Rachel Rising

Photo Credits: Cover Artur Didyk/Shutterstock.com; Cover, p.1 absemetov/Shutterstock.com; Cover, pp.1, 3, 4, 6, 8, 10, 12, 14, 16, 18, 20, 22, 23, 24 StarLine/Shutterstock.com; pp. 4, 8 kamski/iStock/Getty Images Plus; p. 5 Frank Rossoto Stocktrek/Photodisc/Getty Images; p. 7 carebott/E+/Getty Images; p. 9 Mikhail Sidorov/Shutterstock.com; p. 10 Supertruper/iStock/Getty Images Plus; p. 11 THEPALMER/E+/Getty Images; p. 12 avdeev007/E+/Getty Images; p. 13 Cryptographer/Shutterstock.com; p. 14 Jason Todd/Taxi/Getty Images Plus; p. 15 PeopleImages/E+/Getty Images; p. 16 moodboard/Cultura/Getty Images; p. 17 Arthur Mallett/500Px Unreleased/Getty Images; p. 19 Frank Bienewald/Contributor/LightRocket/Getty Images; p. 20 goce/iStock/Getty Images Plus; p. 21 HollenderX2/The Image Bank/Getty Images.

Some of the images in this book illustrate individuals who are models. The depictions do not imply actual situations or events.

Library of Congress Cataloging-in-Publication Data

Names: Rogers, Marie, 1990- author.
Title: ATVs / Marie Rogers.
Description: New York : PowerKids Press, [2022] | Series: Let's ride! | Includes index.
Identifiers: LCCN 2020045772 | ISBN 9781725327313 (library binding) | ISBN 9781725327290 (paperback) | ISBN 9781725327306 (6 pack)
Subjects: LCSH: All terrain vehicles–Juvenile literature.
Classification: LCC TL235.6 .R64 2022 | DDC 629.228/8–dc23
LC record available at https://lccn.loc.gov/2020045772

Manufactured in the United States of America

CPSIA Compliance Information: Batch #CSPK22: For Further Information contact Rosen Publishing, New York, New York at 1-800-237-9932

CONTENTS

ATV ACTION!

Whether you're on the job or the racetrack, you've got to be daring to ride an all-terrain **vehicle**, or ATV for short. The word "terrain" means a type of land. ATVs can travel through woods and over mountains. They can even cross small rivers! An ATV has an engine and usually three or four strong wheels.

Farmers, ranchers, park rangers, rescue teams, and other workers use ATVs. Some people race ATVs. Others just ride for fun, on trails and over hills called sand dunes.

On beaches, lifeguards often use ATVs to get around. If someone gets hurt, ATVs can be used to get them quickly and safely off the beach.

MANY SHAPES AND SIZES

There are many kinds of ATVs. Some have large engines, while others have small engines. ATVs have seats and handlebars like motorcycles. Narrow seats and wide handlebars make ATVs fairly easy to control. ATVs also have lights so riders can see—and be seen—at night.

Most ATVs have either three or four wheels. Three-wheel ATVs are called trikes. Four-wheel ATVs are quads. Both kinds have big, fat tires to help the vehicles go over rocks and uneven ground.

ATV tires are often **flexible** and have low **pressure**. This makes for a softer landing when riding over bumps.

What's What with Wheels?

Three-wheel ATVs were popular in the 1970s and 1980s. They're still sometimes used today. However, three-wheel ATVs can be unsafe because they tip over easily. In 1988, the U.S. government banned new trikes from being sold.

Today, four-wheel ATVs are by far the most popular. They're easy to ride and don't tip over easily. **Professional** ATV riders commonly use them in races.

Though not common, some ATVs have six wheels. These are used mostly for work and for carrying loads.

Three-wheel ATVs like this one are not commonly sold anymore. However, some people build their own three-wheel ATVs.

EARLY ATVS

The first ATV similar to the ones we know today first came on the market in 1970. These three-wheel ATVs were made by the car and motorcycle maker Honda. They had large, balloon-like tires to help with going over bumps. In the 1980s, Honda began putting **shock absorbers** on its ATVs.

In 1983, a carmaker called Suzuki sold the first four-wheel ATV. Soon, more companies started making quads, and they quickly became popular. Today, almost all ATVs are quads!

Many people ride ATVs through the woods for fun. Farmers and hunters also use them for getting around and carrying supplies.

BIG NAMES IN THE GAME

ATVs have many uses. Someone looking to use their ATV for sport will likely buy a different kind than someone looking to use it for utility, or work. The company Yamaha is known for making great sport ATVs. The YFZ and Raptor models are some of the most popular.

Well-liked utility ATV makers include Kawasaki, Polaris, and Arctic Cat. Several companies, such as Suzuki, make ATVs that are good for both sport and utility purposes.

Some ATVs work especially well for riding—or racing!—on sand.

RIDING SAFE

It takes a lot of skill and practice to be able to safely ride an ATV. Every rider needs the right gear, starting with a helmet and strong boots. Racers wear padding that keeps their shoulders and legs safe. They also wear gear called gloves on their hands.

Beginner riders should take an ATV safety course and learn about their ATV. New ATVs come with a small book called an owner's manual. This has important **information** about how to work the ATV.

Goggles are big glasses that fit close to your face. ATV riders often wear them to keep their eyes safe from dirt, mud, and wind.

Where to Ride

Like the name suggests, ATVs can go over all types of terrain, or ground. Many people ride on trails through forests. Some like to ride through large pits of mud, called mud bogs. Others enjoy riding on sand dunes or through open fields.

At racetracks, people called stunt riders do tricks on their ATVs and put on shows for fans. Stunt riders often do backflips or drive their ATVs off giant jumps. Stunt riders have lots of training and practice.

Stunt riders sometimes go to special locations to film extra shocking tricks.

LET'S RACE!

For those who like to **compete**, an ATV race is the place to be. Races take place on tracks made of dirt or mud. The tracks have tight corners and long, straight parts called straightaways. Many have huge jumps too!

Professional racers have teams of **mechanics** who travel with them from race to race, making sure the ATVs are in good shape. But you don't have to be a professional to enter a race. There are different races for people with different skill levels.

The racetrack can get crowded! Crashes can happen. That's why it's important to wear safety gear and follow the rules of the race.

87
212
74
116
9

RIDING OFF!

People should ride ATVs in areas with grass or dirt on the ground. Riders shouldn't take them on **paved** roads. Depending on where you live, there may be other rules or laws about where a person can drive an ATV.

With proper training and safety measures, ATVs can be a great way to enjoy the outdoors. Many popular vacation spots even offer ATVs for rent as a fun activity and **unique** way to see the area. Where would you want to ride?

In the United States, states have their own rules about how old you have to be to drive an ATV. Most people who study ATV safety say riders should be at least 16.

GLOSSARY

compete: To try to win a contest with others.

flexible: Able to bend without breaking.

information: Knowledge obtained from study or observation.

mechanic: A person who builds and fixes machines.

paved: Covered with a matter that forms a hard, level surface, such as a road.

pressure: A force that pushes on something else.

professional: Earning money from an activity that many people do for fun.

shock absorber: A part on a vehicle that makes a ride less bumpy.

unique: One of a kind.

vehicle: An object that moves people from one place to another.

For More Information

Books

Dickmann, Nancy. *ATVs.* North Mankato, MN: Capstone Press, 2021.

Mikoley, Kate. *Off-Road Racing.* New York, NY: Gareth Stevens Publishing, 2020.

Websites

ATV Racing
americanmotorcyclist.com/atv-racing/
Read about some of the biggest ATV races in the United States here.

ATV Safety
kidshealth.org/en/teens/atv-safety.html?ref=search
Be sure to read these ATV safety tips if you plan on riding one day when you're old enough!

INDEX